D1187495

Published by Creative Education
and Creative Paperbacks
P.O. Box 227, Mankato, Minnesota 56002
Creative Education and Creative Paperbacks
are imprints of The Creative Company
www.thecreativecompany.us

Design by The Design Lab
Production by Travis Green
Art direction by Rita Marshall
Printed in the United States of America

Photographs by Corbis (2/Patrice Coppee/Ocean,
Fred Bavendam/Minden Pictures, Dave Fleetham/
Design Pics, Chris Newbert/Minden Pictures, Flip
Nicklin/Minden Pictures, Bernard Radvaner), Getty
Images (Mauricio Handler), Shutterstock (Vittorio
Bruno, Rich Carey, Boris Pamikov)

Library of Congress Cataloging-in-Publication Data
Riggs, Kate.
Octopuses / Kate Riggs.
p. cm. — (Amazing animals)
Summary: A basic exploration of the appearance,
behavior, and habitat of octopuses, the eight-armed
ocean creatures. Also included is a history of the
belief that octopuses were sea monsters.
Includes bibliographical references and index.
ISBN 978-1-60818-613-6 (hardcover)
ISBN 978-1-62832-219-4 (pbk)
ISBN 978-1-56660-660-8 (eBook)
1. Octopuses—Juvenile literature. I. Title. II. Series:
Amazing animals.
QL430.3.O2R54 2016
641.6'94—dc23   2014048709

CCSS: RI.1.1, 2, 4, 5, 6, 7; RI.2.2, 5, 6, 7, 10;
RI.3.1, 5, 7, 8; RF.1.1, 3, 4; RF.2.3, 4

HC 9 8 7 6 5 4 3 2
First Edition PBK 9 8 7 6 5 4 3 2 1

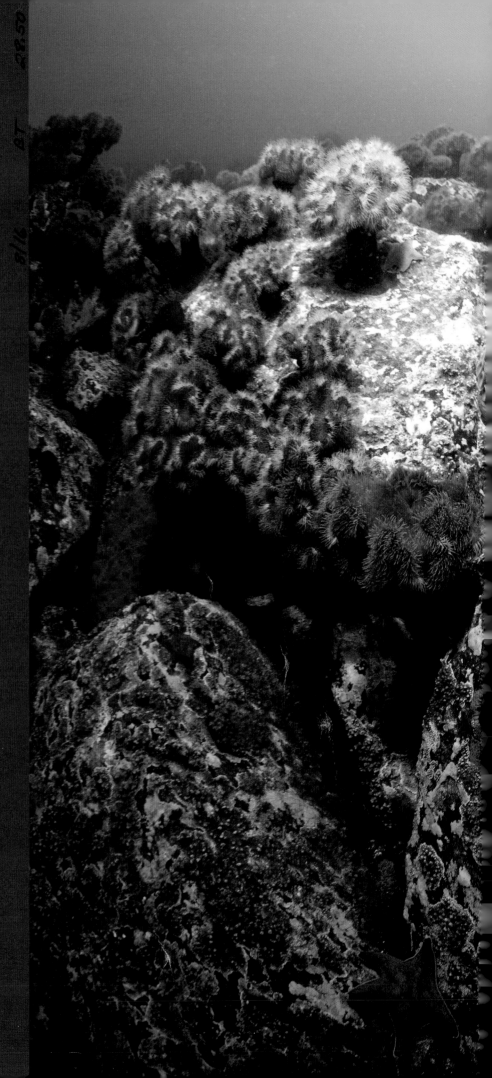

AMAZING ANIMALS

OCTOPUSES

BY KATE RIGGS

CREATIVE EDUCATION • CREATIVE PAPERBACKS

Blue-ringed octopuses live in the Pacific and Indian oceans

Octopuses are animals with ball-shaped heads and flat bodies. They live in salty waters. There are about 300 kinds of octopuses. Dumbo octopuses live in the deepest parts of **oceans**. Common octopuses live in many seas and oceans.

oceans big areas of deep, salty water

All octopuses have eight arms. Rows of suckers are underneath each arm. There are no bones in the octopus's body. The soft flesh that covers the body is called the mantle.

Strong suckers help octopuses grip things in the water

Some octopuses are as small as M&M's. Others are as large as adult humans. The giant Pacific octopus is 16 feet (4.9 m) from the tip of one arm to another.

A day octopus's arms may reach three feet (91.4 cm) across

Octopus arms are webbed.

This helps octopuses move through water. They spend their whole lives in water. Octopuses breathe through gills. They do not need air like some animals do.

Octopuses creep underwater using their arms and suckers

The giant Pacific octopus can pull apart or drill into shells

Octopuses use their suckers to feel and taste. The suckers grip **prey**. Then the arms wrap around the prey like ropes. Octopuses eat animals like crabs, lobsters, clams, and fish. They use their hard beaks to bite prey.

prey animals that are killed and eaten by other animals

Some octopus mothers hang their eggs from the den's ceiling

Female octopuses lay eggs. They may hide their eggs in a **den**. In about 50 days, the eggs **hatch**. Some baby octopuses can swim right away. Others float on top of the water for a while. Babies grow quickly.

den a home that is hidden

hatch come out of an egg

Octopuses live for one to four years. They live alone. They can have babies when they are 6 to 10 months old. After they have babies, octopuses usually die.

Many small baby octopuses get eaten before they grow up

Octopuses shoot big, dark clouds of ink into the water

Octopuses have to take care of themselves. They shoot ink at **predators**. The ink is black, brown, or dark red. It usually scares a predator like an eel or shark. Then the octopus can swim away.

predators animals that kill and eat other animals

People are still finding new kinds of octopuses. Octopuses are good at hiding and changing what they look like. People love to search for these sneaky creatures!

Some octopuses make a hole in the sand or mud to hide

An Octopus Story

Why were people scared of octopuses? Long ago, sailors thought octopuses were sea monsters. They called them "kraken." The sailors thought an octopus could wrap its arms around a ship! Finally, people started catching octopuses to study. The animals are still mysterious, but they are not as scary anymore.

Read More

Lauber, Patricia. *An Octopus Is Amazing*. New York: HarperCollins, 1990.

Wallace, Karen. *Gentle Giant Octopus*. Cambridge, Mass.: Candlewick, 1998.

Websites

Octopus Games and Videos
http://www.learninggamesforkids.com/animal-games-octopus.html
This site has word games and videos about octopuses.

Wild Kratts: Octopus Power!
*http://pbskids.org/video/?guid=00b6423c-da19-4d91-9008
-a9195001c1dc*
Meet a giant Pacific octopus named Georgia.

Note: Every effort has been made to ensure that the websites listed above are suitable for children, that they have educational value, and that they contain no inappropriate material. However, because of the nature of the Internet, it is impossible to guarantee that these sites will remain active indefinitely or that their contents will not be altered.

Index

arms 7, 8, 11, 12, 22

babies 15, 16

eggs 15

gills 11

ink 19

kinds 4, 8, 20

mantles 7

oceans 4

predators 19

prey 12

sizes 8

suckers 7, 12